Still Life with Waterfall

≋

Still Life
with
Waterfall

≈

Eamon Grennan

Graywolf Press

SAINT PAUL, MINNESOTA

Publication of this volume is made possible in part by a grant provided by the Minnesota State Arts Board, through an appropriation by the Minnesota State Legislature, a grant from the Wells Fargo Foundation Minnesota, and a grant from the National Endowment for the Arts. Significant support has also been provided by the Bush Foundation; the Lannan Foundation; Marshall Field's Project Imagine with support from the Target Foundation; the McKnight Foundation, and other generous contributions from foundations, corporations, and individuals. To these organizations and individuals we offer our heartfelt thanks.

Published by Graywolf Press
2402 University Avenue, Suite 203
Saint Paul, MN 55114
All rights reserved.

www.graywolfpress.org

Published in the United States of America
Printed in Canada

ISBN: 1-55597-363-9

2   4   6   8   9   7   5   3   1
First Graywolf Printing, 2002

Library of Congress Control Number: 2001096557

Cover art: Pierre Bonnard, *Sunset* (detail), 1912
© 2002 Artists Rights Society (ARS), New York / ADAGP, Paris
Photograph: © Francis G. Mayer / CORBIS

Cover design: Jeanne Lee

Contents

There is this bubbling before the sun,
This howling at one's ear, too far
For daylight and too near for sleep.

— WALLACE STEVENS, "The Dove in Spring"

At Work

On slow wings the marsh hawk is patrolling
possibility — soaring, sliding down almost to ground level,
twisting suddenly at something in the marsh hay or dune grass,
their autumnal colours snagging his eye
where he finds the slightest aberration, any stir
that isn't the wind's, and abruptly plunges on it.
Then,
if he's lucky — and that scuttling minutiae of skin and innards,
its hot pulse hammering, isn't — he will settle there
and take in what's happened: severing the head first,
then ripping the bright red strings that keep the blood in check,
then eyes, gizzard, heart, and so to the bones, cracking
and snapping each one — that moved so swift and silent
and sure of itself, only a minute ago, in the sheltering grass.

Shock Waves

Sunflower seeds, stone walls, eyes in hiding, phantasmagoria
of the sighted world: I wear white dunes in my eardrums

and it's no world I hear, not even a lust-muffled last echo
when the chambers open and shut, shaking the walls, the boat

of words rising on these shock waves, rising and falling, I feel it,
but hear no syllable of the *slipslapslop* of agitated ocean

across the bow, nor the long telegraph of blue notes that the huge
underwater heart-stoppers use to wreak erotic havoc, each

to each, not the least beat heard where the green bent of branches
and the frantic signing of hemlock to cottonwood

point peremptory directions. *Be,* they sign me; then, *Be other,*
in that *long viduity* of aura, when even breathing — its heavy

spondees measuring the night — disappears, becomes another
nothing in the world, although the soundless heart, celled

in hush like honeybees sleeping, still
does what it has to (composing itself in a constellation of shades)

and stays for a sign out of your small hands, now the enamel-
skinned Adriatic is cracked behind us, the air frothy

and wide-awake with longing, the hard clear stars saying the way.

Agnostic Smoke

Open daisies in the grass, stars in the sky, that half-barrel
and the birds on it, or the silvery steely slateblue skin
of a mackerel: honeycomb of spiderlines and diamonds
and inside in close-up — look! — royal blue. Where do birds go
nights, or buff-colored heifers up to their bellies in buttercups
as they haul as if nothing the great weight of themselves
to lake edge and back, sinking beyond their bony hocks
in the boggy grass, the brushed green rushes making
a sound like raincoats? Nothing but blues of space waiting
my agnostic praise, but from my chimney, too, lord,
the smoke goes up, though this is after rapture,
and the sight of a pheasant crossing the morning garden
briskly, like a man on business, can't trigger whatever
the celebratory nerve was — it's only the eye just looking,
as a tree might look, intending nothing beyond
being there, breaking daylight into little brilliant bits
to become itself in every instant: barked, branched, alive
with leaf-light: countless its ways of being, being like that.

Cold Morning

Through an accidental crack in the curtain
I can see the eight-o'clock light change
from charcoal to a faint gassy blue, inventing things

in the morning that has a thick skin of ice on it,
as the water tank has — so nothing flows, all is bone,
telling its tale of how hard the night had to be

for any heart caught out in it, simple flesh and blood
no match for the mindless chill that's settled in,
a great stone bird, its wings stretched stiff

from the tip of Letter Hill to the cobbled bay, its gaze
glacial, its hook-and-scrabble claws fast clamped
on every window, its petrifying breath a cage

in which all the warmth we were is shivering.

Grid

A deer in the field of morning, tan coat gleaming —
every strand silvered where the sun hit and carded.
He stares till he sees what you are, then a huge
expulsive *whufff* and he's dolphining green waves
to a safer distance, standing solid in shadow
under a chalky, almost transparent half moon
in its baking-bowl of blue, waiting to vanish.

You crane towards top branches to catch
the invisible bird up there, singing in its grid
of anxious moments — throat throbbing, head
uplifted; never any real peace but singing it
anyway. Gravel-steps press your dream: a body
in a red summer dress; sunlight seeing through
till it's only tremor and after-image, nothing.

Not to be carried away in raptures and arrivals
but take the pulse of things, now the photographs
are torched, the undressed daily letters shredded.
Somewhere there's a pressing of pith and skin,
full flesh and stone under the rollers' weight,
loaded again and rolled till the green translucent
drop by drop integrity is found: you dip

your fingers, taste the round sum of sorrow
going home. And soon you might come upon
seriousness for the first time: caught unawares
and belled from the threshold, being fair game.
But now the heart in forecast freezes, although
the words — lovely and fleshful as in the land
of hope — still will out, the shock of truth not yet

an oxygen-ripple in the bloodstorm, reddening it.

Up Against It

It's the way they cannot understand the window
they buzz and buzz against, the bees that take
a wrong turn at my door and end up thus
in a drift at first of almost idle curiosity,
cruising the room until they find themselves
smack up against it and they cannot fathom how
the air has hardened and the world they know
with their eyes keeps out of reach as, stuck there
with all they want just in front of them, they must
fling their bodies against the one unalterable law
of things — this fact of glass — and can only go on
making the sound that tethers their electric
fury to what's impossible, feeling the sting in it.

Bonnard's Reflection

His bedrooms reek of sex and melancholy:
whose leg flexes over a shoulder, whose
hot hand finds a thigh, arms around
the smooth swerves of whose back? We clutter,
he says, and choke. We fail love,
telling all sorts of lies. The whole pink globe
of the cherry tree pressed against one window,
blotting the sky out. Eros erodes us. This
is where *itch* begins to rhyme with *ache:*
one more nail in whose coffin? You'll wait
and see. Flowers on the down comforter
already hissing and whispering what it is
they know to the flowers on the dawn curtain.

Wind Chimes

Thunderhead. Thundercloud.
First a hush in which
the persistent small voices grow
querulous in their immense
present instant, agitated,
waiting for it.

≈

Weeks no sign of the moon
although she's there, buried
above clouds, getting on
and on with her changes.

≈

The feel of fingerbone
when hands are joined
like that and folded: small
flushed hands, olive-mottled.
And going to the door
at intervals: is that thunder?

≈

Drying, things get lighter,
dreaming flight. *Look —
it is evening; look,*
she said, *it is nearly night.*
And *A kiss on the head
wipes away memory.* Meaning,
she meant to say, it didn't.

≈

Now birds sing on little
quiverbranches in my skull
and the manic lark
lights out of my ear
in somersaults of song
where my eyes, God rest them,
are flying. So things
may start to look back at me:
the barrel, the sheep's horn,
even the lake, the reeds, even
the spade, earth-clotted,
leaning against hedge-glow.

≈

Tomorrow, too, will be
the verb "to miss." How it
prises between skin
and skeleton, swims
quick rivulets of blood,
figuring even the way
fingers clutch the pen.

≈

But what is it keeps
the voice in check?
One foot, it is,
nailed to the bedroom floor.
There it goes again —
that silence. So
open your mouth. Spell
"branks." Close slowly now.

Gift

No wind in the world, everything still as a mirror
but facing away from you where you walk
head down, following the tracks in the sand
that are all that's left of the nightstalkers, ghosts now
gone underground with their hunger, hoping dusk
comes soon. Nothing to be seen or heard, the sea
not making the slightest ripple, vacant acres of glass
paving a way to islands that are light blue chimera
adrift on rafts of white mist — as if they were
low clouds, things of light and air only. So it's a gift
to come in the middle of the dunes upon a dark pool
with plant life thriving in it, and to find — to your tongue's
complete surprise — sweet water under its skin of ice.

Rainbow Skirt

Between bars of rain, the table looks out at the bird.
   Wrapped in its own watershawl
the house is pecked at. So the tree comes down.

Days later, limbs lopped, it is a cold blaze
   of amputations — stacked neat as stanzas
in the mist and rain. Terminal spark of sap and sawdust.

Cedar waxwings stop in the top branches. Sit for a slow
   sun-polish to every feather. Lisping music, sipping
sunlight: hordes of small birds hurrying south.

In January — unimaginable! — two bluebirds. Day and night
   he is eating his knuckles
as if there were no tomorrow. Months mooning by. Years.

Sweat-speckled, honeyed at every pore, joined like any other
   couple at the hip: the etymology of grief
seeps into stones that hold the house together.

Crown of gold, rainbow skirt: "She doesn't say anything,"
   says the child, drawing Aphrodite. Paperwhite narcissi
rising from a rack of white stones. Hawk-light. Wind

cuffing water. Lightness of hands, blue veins pencilled in.
   Silver bangle, oxblood boots, bones
of the face: she's all there. *Forget your life. Get up.*

But not yet dawn in her golden, open sandals.

Why?

I like to create a painting round an empty space.
— PIERRE BONNARD

Because space has taken the shape
of her absence; because he wants

to climb down into the mound
of dead leaves steaming and darkening
into November, letting go their ghosts
of chlorophyl, balsam, other woody spices;

because he would do it with the same
solicitude as that Roman family
making their marble farewells to the mother
on death's irreparable threshold;

because every window has a shade in it,
a scarf unravelling into shadowed air;
and because in wakefulness and grief
he has become a moral insomniac —

a crossroads where opposite instincts
keep scratching each other to bits
like blind branches and will soon
wear themselves to nearly nothing,

become a dangling absence, a given
breath, this emptied bed, an echo.

Pulse

Headier than anything distilled or fermented,
shudder-touch of the pulse between her legs
with his flat-open hand on it, taking its small beats
as they tumble after one another one by one,
as a bird inside a hiding place of wet leaves
might give the game away, the whole branch
a spasm asperging suddenly air with light-drops,
silence broken by a faint cry of fright as a hand
bunches and pushes in — fingers bent, extending
their search for softness, wild eyes igniting
as it backs deeper into the dark till it can no more
and in a commotion of flesh and feathering feels
pulse against pulse, and capture, coming to light, release.

Man Making the Bed

Psalm after psalm into a dead sea of silence: they invent
their own enormous, endangered day. Scalded, lord,
by sunlight and the lizards watching, licking dust,

he unfolds the fresh sheets: brisk sniff of laundry, white
as a field of Queen Anne's lace. The word "linen"
comes to rest, a cleansing breath, and a big sail bellies

in the breeze he conjures, speaking its memory of flax and water,
acres of raw linen in the Low Countries or the black North
laid out like a waiting canvas, a picture-glimpse of heaven

with a few shriven women's bodies adrift in it, dazzled
by its dear, old-world, breathing spaces. He billows the sheet
and a wondercloud swells in this small room, a huge

snow-ruffle drifting down, a tabernacle of cool white
rising in the desert. Here is the bed new made, and here
its play of flesh and spirit, unsettling themselves in bodies.

He is alone here, making the bed up, stopped
between the solidity of things as they are and the huge white peace
of the sheet-sail flapping from his hands for a matter of seconds

and subsiding, spread flat, its corners pointed
towards where she leans — half-dressed in memory,
one soft stroke of daylight streaking her spine —

to draw taut the sheet he's holding the other side of
and they snap together, lay flat, tug it tight together
in what looks like a fullness of time and truth

and not plummeting asunder. Lying alone
between the sheets tonight, feeling the clean of them,
their white arms tight about him, he will dream

a wilderness of tents in moonlight: asleep,
they will be shivering a little, as if they felt the stars
press their chill rivets in, or the future

with red eyes whispering to rouse them.

Dinner Hour, December

In little dark-ringed frames of light
the neighborhood is dining: heads nod
to one another; candlelight catches on things —
threads of it snapped by knives and forks,
the glass of water, the wine. No one

is not at home here except the man
walking the block alone and peering in
as if he were a visitor from beyond
and wanted to feast his eyes again
on this picture of felicity, trying to read

the lips winestained and quick in talk,
faces where light plays like a dog
in water — haloes of hair, hands flying.

Fallen Branches

Tree-thickened, the night's a field of fireflies, tiny star-tics
bright as mercury, love-signs in the scented here and now
which the thunder he hears grumbling in the distance
will douse and scatter, drowning leaves and hacking open
the dark with its bombard riverrun body and its white-hot
electric dishevelled wings. Yesterday, he kept finding

fallen bits of branches eaten by weather, by just what is
in earth, in air — breakdown and decay. *Death,* he'll say
from a sanitary distance, but what of the live one
stormed at, brought down, and torn asunder in that full
breath and pulsing — so he has to step back, nothing to say,
wishing the slightly fuzzy sticks of cinnamon fernseed

could be "for to go invisible": he'd sprinkle some
and be among tree-shades, near enough to touch the young deer
sniffing at celandine and bracken, pawing the fallen needles
till the word "ardent" puffs up like dust, along with
"I cannot imagine life without you," although it has already
happened, staunch and solid as any grooved trunk

grappling the under-earth to it with arms of steel
for at least a century, a span in which their own firefly light
is a moment's matter, the merest glimmer gone — as they are
in this cloud of wailing dust and dear wounds aching,
whose mother tongue is silent and scold, is no, is yes.

To Grasp the Nettle

Empty your hands. Shake off even the sweat
of memory, the way they burned

to find the cool indented shell of flesh
at the base of her spine, how they cupped themselves

to hold her head, feeling its weight and bones,
every angle of her face and the arc of each earlobe

finding its place in your palm or at your fingertips,
flesh whispering to flesh in its own dialect; or the way

one of them would creep through the breathlessness
of sleep — the sheer unlikely fact of being there, and there

when the light came back — to come to rest on a breast
or claim a hand or settle a warm spot on her belly

or between stilled thighs. Shake it all off:
for as long as they bear the faintest trace

of such hard evidence against you, your hands
will not be steady and the thing will sting you.

Ash

Silence, the grave neat and tidy for once. Later,
a glass of Powers in the bar, sitting with absence.

Blue aster, he says, *yellow rattle, thyme, trefoil, sea strife* —
to fill the gap. Hearing the unleashed whistle of an oystercatcher,
ears a funnel for whispers and claspings, salt rumours,
depth-charges to where light has winged the skin
of her wrist: *Deep breath now,* she says, *now go on under.*

Resting on a bench beside the dead boy's willow,
he hears the ice crack: thump of a heart turning on itself
and stopping. Under her tongue he imagines taking
the temperature of the soul — where it lurks in some
honeycomb corner, tiny and final as a full stop.

But to live in exile from that breath, all those
rowdy instruments of joy dumbed at once: two faces
fleeing from the mirrorglass.

Birdshaped — colour of turquoise and smoky topaz
and grainy with burial abrasions — this
miniature bottle blown to hold Roman perfume
had to be broken for use, perishable and everlasting.

And only this morning her words were
after-images on the ghost of ash, as near to nothing
as you could imagine — till a light gust out of nowhere
ruffled suddenly the remains of what remained
and blew every last trace away.

Silence

The word "consort," poor penny, keeps coming back.
Raising both arms behind her, she kept stroking her neck

and raising her hair up. For coolness. Meanwhile
he went on asking for water, trying to unparch

his charred throat. For what hasn't been done,
there is this void, a space filled with mourning

in silence, the way an animal or a bird — not knowing
what it is — will fill a space its own size and outline

in the daily world, and will be every moment all that.
"Soul," as we say, may be something like it, a space

that has shaped itself to the shape of what's gone
and not returning. Let's see: should he test all the doors?

Will the locks he's put in place spring open? There is
this distilled thing, gin-light, and the glass is ice.

That, for the moment, takes care of the words. Now
he may sit in silence. He may swallow his tongue.

In the Dunes

When you close your eyes in such a silence
death could come up behind you like an old friend
on tiptoe and touch you and that's that, goodbye
the world. I keep my eyes shut fast in this pure nothing

where sand and hedges are still in no wind at all
(almost a miracle on this sea-rounded tip of things)
and hear nothing at first, nothing, and then — as if
out of the egg of silence — small sounds hatching:

thin fluting of a goldfinch; song sparrow's single note
of warning; in the distance a hawk's cry broken off;
crackle of one twig slipping free of another; the tide's
perpetual faint susurrus, no end to its run-on sentence,

and that dry whisper as the sand in sleep keeps shifting.

Bite Marks

A landslide of palpitations. Nothing to be done
except let go of them and go as directed. First,
bite into the heart and feel the silk-spurt
of blood between tongue and teeth. Then
two halves are howling over the word *asunder*
that someone's written in crimson
on the bedroom mirror. And then the child
is pressing against a door that's swollen
after days of rain and won't open, the wood blindly
sensing wetness, pining for its buried roots
and how, earthed as it was, it stretched
to its content in soft weather, although
the child knows nothing of this, only her own
votive need, the safe arms of rooms, voices
taking her in, explaining everything. And here
is a string of kisses, a scarlet bite-mark
where a fall of hair hardly covers the skin
between earlobe and neckbone, the air alive
with talk, phrases flying like swallows
that flash the semaphore of wing and belly
in city windows. And here too is the bristle
of rage: pain lying out in all weathers, slowly
eroding even memory. They have seen it
and turned away, letting it happen
as if someone else were living their lives,
making the known space strange, the heart
stranger, the open wound close enough
to see it beating — and breathing into it
spit and vinegar; silence; salt.

Amputation

Was it the sudden height and speed of things, that dizzying
spin, wind catching words up, carrying them away?
Sight of the child in the rear-view mirror? Hiding-places
razed or forfeited? Fear of crockery drumming the wall,
and the living-room window in bits? Husband or wife
on fire in a Buddhist rage? Or could it have been the pale
fast-forward photographs of some shuffled-into future —
ardour snuffed out by what the days do, nights passing
in a silence broken only by sighs or, preserve us, snores?
Maybe pain, simple as itself, was enough. Whatever it was,
it put the knife between one warm shuddering and another
of the join where talus and tibia used to articulate
with a leg to stand on, making *Late Songs for Anklebone & Flute*.

Current Events

Smoke and sudden flares. Day fleet as a scent off hedges —
honeysuckle or some thick rot-sweetness of the indigenous dead.

Carpet I'm burning, old dry stuff catching fire: in the morning
a charred place on stones; scatter of ash. One thing pushed up

against another breaks the great silence of the world. Or just
my own slow steps on gravel: in their congregate quiet

the cows stare at me and stare — ears and tails flicking, flickering.
This man, now, leaning up from among the staked beans

has a look I know, although his body has gone beyond us.
On the hill road, a field of bog cotton for binding wounds,

and bog asphodel to lead the likes of us over, eyes closed,
then open on saffron and gold, a fresh kind of light

crinkling the wind. Lethal-lipped, honey-tipped, the little
monstrances of sundew await their shining moment:

they sip, swallow, glinting in cloudlight. Then the sheep
biting hillsides to the bone; a yellowhammer glowing

over a clump of heather; the clack and racket of stones
rounding in water; water splintering over stones —

and the sea in the distance, all that remorseless shiny grinding.

Design

Look how the barrel's rusty hoops
keep the whole thing tight together, each graduated stave
in its cunning place, tasty and functional
the coopering
so nothing buckles or sags asunder.
And see how the olm, salamander of caves —
sightless and transparent
in its life of touch —
is brailling its way, inching along,
instant fingers timid and trusting
nothing in the dark, in the black air
it sips at, although in another life you know
it's a tall creature all cinnabar and gashed emerald,
a gorgeous sun-splash of feathers
falling through the skylight when you're not looking —
up all night as you are, designing amulets
against this and that; facing with naked eyes.

Putting on Rings

My mother looking at her hands:
rubies glittered like fruit-seeds,
the one diamond flashing fire.

≈

Feel of the thing, tiny incumbrance
keeping itself in mind, a comfort
through the day's frayed business

or a mote to trouble the mind's eye:
bird in hand; bargain
bearing lightly on the flesh.

≈

As if by memory or instinct, your hands
go thoughtlessly about the task
while your eyes are elsewhere:

a cry from the child's bedroom
or weather looming through the window
or a face in the mirror, another pair of eyes.

≈

Purposeful, brisk, quotidian,
quickest of ceremonies, agent of change,
a notion of the soul —

which may itself be nothing
but a ring, an airy nothing
circled and closed off by light.

≈

Hard to miss
the implicit sex of it,
as if the two of you

could stay all day like that,
knowing openness
and enclosure — being contained.

≈

Everyday grace of it:
how one hand holds the other
like an old friend, putting on

this figure of fullness, but discreet
as walking to the window
and drawing blinds.

≈

Lightweight wonder —
a sort of bandage
for some soul-wound or another,

for the niggling void
that nothing
can quite fit or obliterate.

≈

Now my mother's rings
are on other fingers,
but her wedding-band

is in the grave — the merest whisperglint
clinging to fingerbone: stubborn sign
of what she was and wanted.

≈

Putting one on,
how you feel at first
a whisper of chill

licking your skin —
until the ring
is the very temperature

your blood is.

Butterfly, Breath, Small Birds

Butterfly in tar: a stained-glass fossil.
And this laurel tree, green all winter —
ramifying, dreaming households.
Heart-ice, cloudlight, geese floating over:
whose future in their feathered bones?
Bloodbeat and heart-thump steady as they go.

Breasts and everything on show,
but it's the pierced right ear
he finds his eye going back to. Room so cold
they could see their breath at blood-heat
frosting the windowpane,
blinding its clear unlying eye.

Two small birds in the leafless ginkgo:
through steelblue chill their pure
antiphonal whistling. Then a sudden
shuddering warmth: his jacket, her arms
around it. He's inside somewhere, feeling
each button, knuckle, lips that tilt away.

Such sharp song they had, and clean green throats.

Eye Trouble

Not clear exactly what to do to clear the eye,
sandpaper away from that tender membrane
what has settled on it — crust of unknowing,
crust of the single fixed idea, crust of the image
that won't lift or dissipate, like the fog
that eats the mountain here for days, high, no, low
as the sloped roof of this one-storey cottage
and nothing, no cleansing breath or freshened light,
can pierce it. So how scour the thing? Name
the burn, blade, reaming-knife or melting acid
that will take away what sticks there tight
as one leaf of skin cleaves to another while
the flesh is mending, its cut slowly closing.

Sitter, Renvyle

Sitting outside when the sun comes back, I hold up my throat
to its open blade: soundwaves
crest at my sleepy ears, leaving their flotsam of birdsong
and tractors ticking over, the long clean line of bee-sound,
and that sudden, highpitched, rasp-blue riff
of a bluebottle — or the syncopation of two
builders' hammers, or this watery breeze-in-leaves, or that
clicketing wren, tapping its frantic Morse.

Blessing of a break in bad weather that lasted and lasted,
the sudden good day settling around me
like a tame linnet lighting on my heated shoulder,
singing and staying there with no fear in the world
as time itself rolls back and lets me in on its secret,
that for the moment
it has folded its tent and taken to the air
and dissolved in it, so there's time
to catch the discreet throat-clearing *hhackk!*
of the approaching pheasant, time to read
the spiral-script of white lichens on the rock
or the duff-green cover of moss
on big stones that curve their backs
above the undulant, elemental grass — like dolphins.

Sitting like this, I know the shade of the east-facing cottage
will find me soon with its chill
and usher me out
into the domain of digitalis, cuckooflower, scabious, vetch,
out into the blue-roofed kingdom of larks
that electrify the air and stand on the wind — artists
of their own furious, musical repose. Out there,
in and out of the ancient passage grave

and between its stately great upended stones
fly stonechat and starling, wheatear and blackbird,
rose-chested linnet, chaffinch, wren — in and out
of the burial court of great men in their time, these live birds
who know nothing of the space we share
but what their beaks and airy bones tell them,
and their lit, quicksilver eyes.

Killing the Bees

They'd been there for years, secreted in the ceiling
of the back bedroom — between sealed rafters, plaster
and roof boards — making their own music, leading
a life blind to all but their native needs
and cycles. It couldn't last: armed, masked
under a cloud of sacking-smoke, we knocked a hole
into their cells, sowing anger and panic, a sound
we had, amazed, to shout over, masses of bodies
blackening the light-bulb, a live stalactite of honey
spiralling gold to the floor, the fumes we sprayed
killing them in their thousands. What survived
we dragged outside, drenched in petrol, put a match to,
dug a pit for. Bedroom a battlefield, bodies thick in it.

Windowgrave

The dead bee lies on the window-ledge, a relic,
its amber-yellow body barred in black and its head

tucked in, dust gathering on every follicle
and on the geodesic dome of the head — all tucked in

and tucked away, so neat is death. And the many
flies too, all sizes, lying on their sides as if

asleep, just a quick nap and they'll be up and off
about their business. *Souls,* we used to say:

bees, butterflies, moths, wasps, all sorts of flies,
the air crowded and loud with leftover angels —

but not the spider in its complex web, fallen
from grace but walking on air, vigilant in ways

that harden the heart, getting its appetite back.

Caterpillar and Dancing Child

It isn't only the child in the head it is,
but this one who dances her life for us —
turning like a miniature pillar of fire
before us, spinning on the tip of her toes
and spinning, taking the milk to the kitchen.
Or who'll float one step at a time
up the stairs to bed, or pirouette in the mirror
to see how her hair is, translating her life
into such speechlessness, full of herself
and the joy of it, moving, moving,
or who'll open our ears, amazed, to the sound
of her singing a hymn of angel-bread
in Latin, till the house fills with it,
the bread flies from the table,
and the flowering crown-of-thorns in the corner
twists light into itself, as if in scarce earth
it could live forever — forever bright-eyed
in this house of cards where the cat
is scooped up by a small pair of arms
and forced close to our hearts.
                              Yesterday
I missed by inches crushing a caterpillar
underfoot in the spring-lit garden: exact
as a Japanese lacquered box, it was
black-bodied, fringed, white-streaked,
with tiny turquoise eyes on its flanks
and legs the colour my beard was once,
and I watched it ripple through grass-stems,
driven by the one leaf that speaks
to its hunger, where it eats its fill and flows
over a wilderness of grit, bright mica morsels
marking its way — not at the speed of light

but in the arms of it, putting one foot
in front of the other and covering
the ground as we do — towards that
deep undreaming sleep in which
it will become, as our child is, a life dancer.

Vermeer, My Mother, and Me

Roof and sky and chimney stacks,
the blue, the white, the reddish browns —
how he might have seen Westfield Road
and the coppergreen spires of Mount Argus
from the window of my childhood bedroom

I can gather from a little corner
of his *Little Street,* and the almost
unremarkable presence in it
of the woman bent over in her own back yard,
who is leaning for a mop in a wooden bucket

and who just might be my mother
at our kitchen door, her eyes cast down
to the shore that's clogged and stinking again
as she takes in a breath — filled
with the smells of grass and apples,

coal dust, Jeyes Fluid, and the sugary
toffee scent from the factory down the road —
that will, when she raises her head,
come out with my name on it, my own
two syllables making their instant way

back through the kitchen, along the narrow hall,
up the dark-carpeted stairs and into
the small, wallpapered, big-windowed bedroom
where I'll hear that name and her known voice
shaping it, making it quick, making me

be there, myself in the very moment
when our daily life — defined
by cloud-broken blue sky and the ginger
bricks of gable-ends, radiance of roof-tiles
and wet chimneys — has to happen, there

where she's calling me to come, quick, help her.

Enough

First thing I saw near dawn on the road to the dunes this morning
was, at last, the fox: just a quick glimpse of him on the run

but enough to see his colour is the colour of marsh hay
in this season — copper and ginger streaked with slatey black —

and enough to see his ears, plump sides, rump and bushy tail
vanishing into a twisted cave of tree roots

between some houses and the salt marsh where he's left
line after line of his impressions for me to follow,

easier in my mind now, having seen his real presence
ignite like that — the beautiful slow burn of it

as he steps from my sight into his own tangle of shadows —
and not having to content myself with the marks only

of his absence: the smell of him, his neat prints filling with sand.

White Water

Yes, the *heart aches,* but you know or think you know it could be
indigestion after all, the stomach uttering its after-lunch cantata
for clarinet and strings, while blank panic can be just a two-o'clock
shot of the fantods, before the afternoon comes on in toe-shoes
and black leotard, her back a pale gleaming board-game where all
is not lost though the hour is late and you've got light pockets.

There is a port-hole of light at the end of the hemlock tunnel:
birds cross it, flashing their voices at you, and you feel —
from the way they tilt their heads and their throats swell —
the beat of their brief song, another sign the world is what it is:
a shade-tree heavy with households, its fruit for meat, its leaf
for medicine. But that business of the first kiss is hard to fathom:

knees quaking, white water over broken rock, and the coracle
you trusted your life to in a bit of a spin, head swimming
with the smell of flesh so close you feel it breathing, spilling secrets —
its inmost name, for one, and what the near future feels like, time
wobbling to a tribal thing without tenses, and that tenacious "I"
a thing of the past, only a particle of the action now, nothing

separate, *a luminous tumult,* an affair of air and palate, air
and larynx, tongue, throat, teeth, whatever brings the words out
in their summer dresses — and you can hear the crow's black
scavenger guffawing, egg- and offal-scoffer, comedian of windspin,
so all of a sudden you rush your kingdom-come, the two of you,
insects shedding your dry, chitinous skins. And although what's left

is raw for a while, the slightest breath burns it, in time it comes
to become you, you can live into it, intoning the Sebastian koan —
whose who in pain, who's who? — and know, or close-to-know,
the *here it is:* two clean rooms in the next parish to wholeness.

After Rain

See how our big world turns tiny and upside down
in raindrops on thorns of gorse: along the lane
to the small harbour the hedges are empty of leaves
and everything has a flayed, scrubbed look, antique
and about to be new, the brusque wind flailing branches,
declaring change, a change in the weather
that must unsettle us, too, who persist inside its loops
and mazes, unable to see straight, unable to forecast
tomorrow or the day after, only able to remember
what happened: the air scenting to freshness, a sense
of calm coming down, of getting to the other side
of turbulence, of things being touched for once
to wholeness; that somehow nothing bad could happen.

Signs

1

When high tide happens
and the Hudson comes to a full stop for a moment —
massive slabs of ice at a standstill —
and the upstream push of the Atlantic
runs out of steam,
and gravity's feedback to the sea
hasn't started
to take the river in its beak
and bring it back to Manhattan,
I believe I know something
of the feel of it. Wall
of fire, wall of glass,
bridges burning. *Only yesterday*
we were in love.

2

Uncertainly there, but there,
smell of lindens after rain,
then nothing
but heaped earth, fallen branches,
the animal
scrabbling to survive.
Blood roaring, going cold.
Threshold gaze:
edgy, the eyes make out
the shape a woman prints
on the clothes she wears.
A body burning
like the word "Venice" in the singer's mouth.

Brain cells sizzling for a minute
in real time.

3

Huddle of that couple
on barstools, saying
whatever, tongues in ears.
And then again gone. *Mystery
is all vowel:* might I unlearn myself
back to a few untutored howls,
a hibernating cry in the night,
then take dictation — one hand
over your crumbling eyes, the other
madly scribbling under the table,
ears cocked to the clock
coughing in the hall?

4

Such a fine line connects
the pubic hair in the mirror
to the angel coming in the window.
Dusky scent of you — there
between earlobe and that
vein in your neck.
Again the pale face
stepping out of the rainy morning:
*I can no longer
tell which of us is absent.*
Bone by small bone
you start to unravel:
flesh folds back. Last to go,

the skin I've run my tongue
all over. But always
out at the edge of earshot
lurks thirst — still whispering —
every word a blazing
grain of sand, bite of salt.

Palpitations

If you lie very still, like a spotted newt in shadow,
maybe it won't know you're there, maybe
it will flap on over, maybe its eye will blink
at the right instant, maybe it will not smell
your fear, maybe the nervous waves of air
will stay unruffled, smooth, not break over you,
not tell all there is to know by that sudden
spritz of foam they spit at any impediment. Don't
breathe — that's it — don't let the wind in your chest
set the whole heave of it waving, the way grass
becomes a pale mane running under the hand
of any breeze that beckons. Be the girl who leans
in her horse's ear and whispers, *Easy now, easy.*

Bonnard's Mirror

Vehement spices, a prodigal fog of them.
And lightning flashing its albatross wings,
thunder coming to rattle their bones. Then

the still small voice of the perfume she wore
is beating its tiny fluorescent fists
and turning him inside out again, his eyes

on the figure fixed in the painted mirror,
framed and then framed again
with her head missing. A ripe brown berry

centres the swell of the breast; a line
slides from one nipple down her side
and shadowed thigh — shadowdark thickening

where both thighs must touch each other.
Seeking anywhere to settle, his gaze falls
on what's painted outside the glass: a jug

and basin; bathroom bottles, scents, ointments:
a tiled still life where she might still
be standing among soaps, toothpaste, perfume,

and not losing her head at all
but giving him, caught in the picture with her,
the full force of her open smile

and the matching candour of her body,
the lithe, droplet-glinting quick of it,
as if she'd rise and fly if he didn't hold her

there in the show they've made of themselves —
twinned and stilled like that for a flash
in the looking-glass, but feeling the real light

light on bare heads and steaming shoulders.

Near Dawn

The world in silhouette. A sketching of trees.
Trunks and stripped branches in fretted outline
against faint streaks of almost blue to the east.

Dark cross of a phone-pole on the hill; smoky
shape of Maolchnoc a colossal turf-reek
in the distance. Nearer, through flayed hedges
edging the garden, a car-light is a firefly flicker
in the lingering contest of light and dark.

"A moving mist" is what Traherne calls us,
and when I stand by the fuchsia bush — aching
from yesterday's labour, memory's long haul,
and all the aftershakes of dreamlife — I know
how right he is: we live in silhouette, a shivering.

Anti-Psalm

Where not so much as dreams of light may shine,
Nor any thought of greenness, leaf or bark.
— HENRY VAUGHAN

Big transit of clouds, small transit of birds through the garden.
    Beside the neolithic stones a post transporting electricity.
Then turn that last corner and there it is again, a sea of light.
    And still the world looking back, speaking in tongues,
and a few windows open in the grass, there, under my eyes
    outside my window, windshaken as I am
inside a local corner of the weather, reading psalms. Sunday morning:
    no coffee, no oranges, but a fry of rashers, eggs, sausages,
and the broken coast-lights weathersmacked. I might be standing yet
    beside the empty phone-box, sound of my heart in my mouth
a steady racket, balking again from nearness,
    warm of one cheek against the warm of another.
Constant this turning away: away from the withered hand,
    the eyebrows of malice, the widow's morning sickness,
the splinter-ache called *daughter* at the tip of my tongue.
    But elsewise: quick curl of smoke, a breath, and in the dust
at my bare feet a little pile of words — feathers that rise and fly
    with the next breath, a century or so later.

Vespers

1

At dusk
things take on a light-life
of their own: greens glow, whites shine,
the browns grow black, the *silky*
crisped lakewater gleams
wine-tinted violet. The gravel spectrum
is charcoal to pale beige.
With her heart in her mouth she's dancing,
and her mother, too. A shadowbird
breaks what light is left,
crossing the window. The music stops.
Night melts, dragging its dreams.
Cat got your tongue?

2

Untutored,
a young chaffinch simply sits — almost
invisible on gravel — taking the world in
that is all other. Blink of an eye.
The world. Again. Blink
of an eye. The ash tree
wearing its jerkin of moss.
And they go on
making their songs: all around,
the armies running at one another.
Rice wine, plum petals, cuckoo calling
kuei ch'u. Sick for home.

3

The body
carries on to its own borders:
In night rain
pull up spring onions, steam them
fresh with yellow millet.
I watch her go
slowly from sight: light
on her bare legs, in her hair.
Hushings, glimmerings, half-heard things
lacking a name. To be caught out
in a surf of rain. At eye-level again.

4

Hopkins again. Bless me, Father.
May 5 1868: Cold. Resolved
to be a religious. Cobalt
and Indian red. Mantegna's
draperies. The all
unbuckled. Back to this, then:
nutshell
of infinite space; cloudsphere;
eyelights flying through glass.
Try to make the most, no,
the least of it:
ragged robin, bog orchid, asphodel, yes,
under your nose. Just before —
in a surge of insurge —
your boot flattens them.

Full Moon

Clouds curdle round it, crack open, let it through.
Radiance shaded by cloudshapes; fat fruit
of incandescence; sphere of peeled silver. I wonder

what living by such light would be: soft
collusion of moonshine with grey gables; walls
in a whitewashed trance; argentine grass; twigs

limned in pewter. Ambition and rage all faded
from the air, the air subdued to a new sense
of self, something intimate and sure about the way

it whispers subtle truths neighbour to neighbour —
or how its ashen luminescence slides inside things
so they shed the cinder skin of what goes on

day by day in daylight, and start breathing.

Shepherd to the Wind

The sheep skeleton in the stream
resembles the inside of a small harpsichord
or the sounding-board
of some ancient many-stringed instrument
we've lost the name for, though not
the ten-stringed harp of David
playing "Shepherd to the Wind."

I set some water on the sill
so I can see the warp of the world through it;
otherwise I lead a normal life
pasted to the rockface, trying to feel my way
fingertip by fingertip beyond being,
beyond the word "pitfall" and all it conjures.

In you alone, he says, *the soul can rest.*
Imagine they are holding hands
over the waterfall — the little one, a local wonder —
as the smoke from the last bridge they've burnt
begins to travel, and the heat
of her clean ankle increases, he can feel it,

and conversation begins again
to soak up both their lives — while swarms
of garden gnats perform their blind dance
of zigzag, scribble, and pulsation,
miming the way matter itself
might be: restless specks
of luminous wounded music
in this enchanted void.

Aubade

Walking Renvyle strand at sun-up, I see a gull
that's in the right place at the right time

turn to a bird of fire. And here on a slope of sand
I see an otter must have had to scramble, his big foot

dragging, his unwavering concentration stapled
to the prey he must be — I want to say — *imagining,*

its flesh and blood a little persistent detonation
in his brain, the salt-blue hugeness of the Atlantic

only a cloak he wears at dusk and dawn. *Thereness*
is all: that burn of chance, quickened breath of appetite

adding up to all that this world offers —
glitter and shadow, pang of absence, the way

this day keeps coming on: we meet; we disappear.

Afterweather

And the light comes from nowhere.
— WISLAWA SZYMBORSKA

Begin with the story of rain or Leopardi's sea of *rien*
where the lady surfaces and finds her way to us.
Something touches my shoulder: flipflap of wings
or wind in the grass. A creature with red eyes
flying from smoke, throat closing. Now the garden

is a square of air, leaf-sound where breeze is, smell
of meadowsweet, rosemary; song of a bullfinch
on a branch, then gone — mocker of windowsills.
Empty honeycomb: words inching out of turbulence
the way morning bodies move from room to room

and stare out after storm at the battered trees that
hold their own brand of whimpering, composing
broken notes about the weather. Then open the old door:
eyes fountaining on the known threshold, and day
ticks by on rusted hinges, still trying to sing. Look:

this pouring-in of green, then night. Flayed branches,
daylight moon a fading ghost. Plainchant
is what I'm after: the way it goes on. Storm again,
and a sky scarfed with blue. Pale faces pasted
to the window: I fear for these young ones — bareheaded,

at the mercy of every weather. And wonder how far
the word "longing" will take us. Morning again,
brisk with birds. Two clouds kissing, dissolving. *Soul,*
she says, *is a word for something about the body.*
And now remember what the cloud came to, shading

the dry lake-bed they wakened by. The way things
darkened quickly, as if somehow the season — for all
its freedoms — had a will of its own and could twist
clement weather from them. And when finished
with them — how it had soaked them to the skin.

Encounter

The lake that was caked ice is ice no more,
but waves scudding and making foam, although
if you plunged your arm in up to the elbow
you'd touch the hard table-truth of ice, under which
brown trout tell their own story. A man with a gun

patrols the shore: be not a woodcock or a snipe
this rainy afternoon, or — if you are — sit still as stone
while his spaniel noses the drenched heather. Still,
he says, he'd never shoot a pheasant, "For aren't there
only a few about, the lovely creatures." We stand

for a cigarette, his gun cracked open, and in his hand
two cartridges of shot (wine-coloured, with gold
bands closing them) lie, like matching rings.

Landscape with Teeth

Cattle dusk-sculpted on a plinth of skyline.
Breast of chaffinch a watered strawberry.
Inishturk a whale-shape on the glazed sea.

Bog, clod, soggy, sod, plod. Nimbus
of light over boggy pasture; couchgrass
in flattened mats; blunt push of mushrooms

through loamy hush. Nests, passage graves,
crosses. Steam-clouds out of the cows'
rosy mouths. Soft furnaces of their body-bulk.

Three girls moving through rainmist
under a huge blue umbrella, waiting for Monet
to paint them as they are on the headland:

grey swell of sea, horizon a pale lapis, sky
chequered with cloud; a pointillist silvering
shiver of rain. Their poppy-coloured laugh.

Indoors, a window-ledge of books, that umber
Italian vase of meadowsweet and loosestrife,
a spray of fuchsia against the verdigris

and plumblue bulges of Tully Mountain.
In the foreground one rusted sickle, a single
blip of sunlight igniting its bent tip.

But where do the real dreams come from
in their primary colours — with their small teeth
sharpened and their warm wet tongue?

Painter's Diary

Notations only. Dog-star weather. Marble tiles. Shutters.
A vase of marigolds glowing in the dusk. Dark outline
of a leg-curve. Flesh-coloured streak of arms. Hedges
lemon-blue. Spheres of gleam where trees were, or a razor's
telling edge of light at the door jamb. One smudged hand
holding a cut pomegranate. On the mirrored tablecloth
he finds the *broken white* of a dress and its bone-coloured
buttons. Half-open doors. Silver twist of olive leaves
after rain. Flesh under water. Eyes behind glass. Thirsty
cloudburst of azure grapes. Soon enough, he thinks,
they're dust. But just look at them — shining now
in the great breath of things and night coming. A gathering
of light and air. A mouth. Dusk-glow. Gold of marigolds.

Claim

To lay claim to something, even
this old half-barrel, its rusty
hoops and painted staves
weather-bleached, two streaks
of birdshit brightening its side.
Or bodies stretched to their limit
in that incessant present
they'd stumbled on, falling
forward with small cries of pain,
calling back the long vowels
and that short clamoring they'd entered —
riding air, eager for it, swimming
into the open mouth. A swallow
inhales the garden's air,
and ragged bushes show at once
their bones and bright flowers,
their leafy summer-swollen plenitude
taking the wind in
to sigh its big life among them —
wave after wave
gathering, greeting, going on —

where he sits, almost singing
the praises of shelter, trying
to fathom what it is that squints
in hedge-windows
or on the edge of cloud, or what
among the agitated leaves
the wind insists
to high branches. Clouds, too,
he can see them
shift in their drifting figures

as they marshal and disperse:
their weight unimaginable, almost
on fire with themselves — coasting
towards change and change about
in such bodies, maybe, as angels
might borrow, spreading themselves
in light and through it
or turning all to tears
while the mountains
like immense gentle animals
lie down under the hand
of light itself, and are settled by it.

Hare

. . . the mountain grass
Cannot but keep the form
Where the mountain hare has lain.
— W. B. YEATS

Suddenly there, again, as if drawn out of the windy air,
the hare grazes the grass in front of the livingroom window
and stops at intervals to gaze unseeing in my direction, ears
anxiously flicking, and its eyes (the colour of Concord grapes)
finding who knows what in the world we share, the white
hairs of its chin shivering in the breeze. Suddenly there

to nibble the good grass of the present moment (one green
strand dangling) it's as if it were there always — like the souls
I imagined alive at the other side of mirrors, so when I looked
in at myself they'd see me looking, feel the bond unbroken
between us. Now, when I glance out again, it's gone —
hunkered into absence without a trace, although I know

it will be back, passing in a heartbeat through the wishful mirror.

(in memory of Liam Hourican)

With Skeleton and Shoes

White ticking of the cricket in the grass. Companionable
answering. Two whispering like that as long as you listen.

Gull skeleton filling with sand: ribcage a basket of bone and air
to keep a cricket in, or a green grasshopper with cinnamon legs.

Fluctuant cloud, your blood, the drift of a woman's thighs
crossing a corridor in the opposite direction. Too late for eyes

or faces: the rest is famine. In a darkness full of stars and children
you're learning the names: fairytales of design where none is,

although immediately we see it. Smears of light. Sensualities
of shade. Heart of cloud is limestone, the rim a radiance.

Whole day in front of the window watching wind-driven birds:
the way the grass, the leaves, are nodding and touching.

Today the wind, southeast, has warm hands — hundreds of them
laying about you, surprising skin and bone. Remember

how things were inhabited? Learning the word made flesh, meeting
Vincent's Franciscan shoes. Dazzle-amber of the shirt you wore. And at dusk

a breathing field of cows: body language of mother and child —
muzzle nuzzling neckflap; quick bright flesh-flash of tonguelick.

Country Road

Scarlet mask, copper wings: to be wakened from a dream —
    a woman singing Mozart's *Requiem* — by the dawning
cockcarracarouse of the anemone-cheeked bird
    shouting his foreign heart out. Two fried duck eggs
stain my plate to a painter's palette: deep golden yolk
    drawing fire from the window. Meantime the day
grows porous, turning light inside out, into a shade
    with no name, the way someone may paint a hedge
of blackberries or a narrow country road that's empty
    except for this momentary slanted light, with mulberry-
coloured roof-tiles in the distance. Mid-afternoon
    and nothing there, and he paints it into his journal of loss:
matte grey sky, black evergreens, water-gloss — all
    a backdrop only. Now the longest day
is closing down: a bat-breath brushes my hair; a blackbird
    dashes jabbering at the garden. In this big
wing-spreading silence, little to believe, less to hang onto —
    simply different registers of grass and tree bark, hedges
dimming, a glimmer of gravel, and the sky like
    faded rice paper. Relax, she says, and take in if you can
these drenched buttercups, dripping fuchsias,
    even the rain with that seeming sourceless glow
inside it. But take nothing for granted, not even this
    North African orange that sends its own probe
of sunshine into the cloudy room, scorching
    the walls. So, when the weather is — as it mostly is —
wet and windy, I'll stay indoors over a book, leaning
    closer and closer as light dwindles, to scan it
by that peculiar sheen of rain-light and leaf-light
    and stone-light leaching through the big window.

Detail

I was watching a robin fly after a finch — the smaller bird
chirping with excitement, the bigger, its breast blazing, silent
in light-winged earnest chase — when, out of nowhere
over the chimneys and the shivering front gardens,
flashes a sparrowhawk headlong, a light brown burn
scorching the air from which it simply plucks
like a ripe fruit the stopped robin, whose two or three
cheeps of terminal surprise twinkle in the silence
closing over the empty street when the birds have gone
about their own business, and I began to understand
how a poem can happen: you have your eye on a small
elusive detail, pursuing its music, when a terrible truth
strikes and your heart cries out, being carried off.

Notes

"Shock Waves": The phrase "long viduity" is taken from Beckett (*Krapp's Last Tape*).

"Rainbow Skirt": The sentences in italics are from the poet Rumi, in the Coleman Barks translation.

"White Water": I borrowed the phrase "a luminous tumult" from the Canadian poet, Dennis Lee.

"Signs": The phrase "Mystery is all vowel" appears in the writings of Giorgio Agamben.

"Vespers": The passage in italics, and other incidentals in Parts 2 and 3, are from the Chinese poets, Li Po and Tu Fu, in the translation by Arthur Cooper. The phrases in italics as well as other items in Part 4 are from the *Journals* of Gerard Manley Hopkins.

"Shepherd to the Wind": The phrase in italics is from Saint Augustine's *Confessions.*

"Afterweather": The sentence in italics is Nietzsche's.

"Painter's Diary": Some of the things mentioned are taken from the work of Pierre Bonnard.

"With Skeleton and Shoes": The phrase "Vincent's Franciscan shoes" occurs in Rilke's *Letters on Cézanne*; it is a reference to van Gogh.

Acknowledgments

To the editors of the following magazines, where early versions of many of these poems (some of them with different titles) appeared.

The Gettysburg Review: "Agnostic Smoke," "Windowgrave"

Hayden's Ferry Review: "Wind Chimes," "Current Events," "Claim" [as "Inventory"]

The Irish Times: "Full Moon," "Hare"

The Kenyon Review: "To Grasp the Nettle," "Shock Waves"

Kestrel: "Near Dawn"

Meridian: "Bonnard's Mirror"

Metre: "With Skeleton and Shoes," "Amputation," "Landscape with Teeth," "Why?"

New Hibernia Review: "Pulse," [as *Cuisle*] "Fallen Branches," "Grid" [as "Fixed Stars"], "Bite Marks"

The New Republic: "Anti-Psalm," "Gift"

The New Yorker: "Bonnard's Reflection," "Encounter," "Up Against It" [as "Desire"], "Man Making the Bed," "Vespers," "In the Dunes," "At Work" [as "Artist at Work"]

The Shop: "Design" [as "Amulet"]

NZ: "Shepherd to the Wind," "Design"

Ontario Review: "Putting on Rings"

Poetry: "Aubade," "Enough"

Poetry Ireland Review: "Palpitations," "White Water," "Caterpillar and Dancing Child," "Country Road"

Rattapallax: "Ash"

Shenandoah: "Dinner Hour, December," "Killing the Bees," "Sitter, Renvyle"

Tabla: "Butterfly, Breath, Small Birds"

Thumbscrew: "After Rain"

Times Literary Supplement: "Cold Morning," "Detail" [as "Lesson"]

TriQuarterly, "Ash" [in early version, as "After-Image"]

The Yale Review: "Afterweather"

"At Work" [as "Artist at Work"], "Bite Marks" [as Approximation VII, part II], "Detail" [as "Lesson"], and "Palpitations" [as "Heart Attack"] appeared in *Poets of the New Century*, eds. Roger Weingarten, Richard Higgerson, Jack Myers (David R. Godine, 2001).

"To Grasp the Nettle," and "Claim" [as "Inventory"] received Pushcart Prizes (2001, 2002).

Grateful thanks to the John Simon Guggenheim Foundation and to the MacDowell Colony.

EAMON GRENNAN is an Irish citizen, the Dexter M. Ferry, Jr. Professor of English at Vassar College, and the 2002 Heimbold Professor of Irish Studies at Villanova University. His previous books include *What Light There Is & Other Poems*, *As If It Matters*, *So It Goes*, *Relations: New & Selected Poems*, and *Leopardi: Selected Poems*, a work of translation, and *Facing the Music*, a collection of essays on modern Irish poetry. Grennan is the recipient of fellowships from the Guggenheim Foundation and the National Endowment for the Arts. His work has appeared in many Irish and American publications, including the *New Yorker*, *Poetry Ireland Review*, the *Nation*, *Poetry*, and the *Threepenny Review*.

The text of the poems has been set in Janson, a typeface designed by Miklós Kis who became a major figure in Dutch typography as well as in his native Hungary. He spent most of the 1680s in Amsterdam where he learned the craft.

Book design by Wendy Holdman
Composition by Stanton Publication Services, Inc., St. Paul, Minnesota
Manufacturing by Hignell Book Printing on acid-free paper

Graywolf Press is a not-for-profit, independent press. The books we publish include poetry, literary fiction, and cultural criticism. We are less interested in best-sellers than in talented writers who display a freshness of voice coupled with a distinct vision. We believe these are the very qualities essential to shape a vital and diverse culture.

Thankfully, many of our readers feel the same way. They have shown this through their desire to buy books by Graywolf writers; they have told us this themselves through their e-mail notes and at author events; and they have reinforced their commitment by contributing financial support, in small amounts and in large amounts, and joining the "Friends of Graywolf."

If you enjoyed this book and wish to learn more about Graywolf Press, we invite you to ask your bookseller or librarian about further Graywolf titles; or to contact us for a free catalog; or to visit our award-winning web site that features information about our forthcoming books.

We would also like to invite you to consider joining the hundreds of individuals who are already "Friends of Graywolf" by contributing to our membership program. Individual donations of any size are significant to us: they tell us that you believe that the kind of publishing we do *matters*. Our web site gives you many more details about the benefits you will enjoy as a "Friend of Graywolf"; but if you do not have online access, we urge you to contact us for a copy of our membership brochure.

www.graywolfpress.org

Graywolf Press
2402 University Avenue, Suite 203
Saint Paul, MN 55114
Phone: (651) 641-0077
Fax: (651) 641-0036
E-mail: wolves@graywolfpress.org

Other Graywolf titles you might enjoy are:

Relations: New & Selected Poems
by Eamon Grennan

The Half-Finished Heaven
by Tomas Tranströmer, selected and translated by Robert Bly

The White Lie: New and Selected Poetry
by Don Paterson

Eat Quite Everything You See
by Leslie Adrienne Miller

Bellocq's Ophelia
by Natasha Trethewey